Happy
Day

Dad.

To Treasure Our Days

Marjorie Holmes

To Treasure Our Days

A Celebration of Woman's Role

As Wife, Mother and Friend

Selected by Marianne Wilson

Illustrated by Eve Reddin

HALLMARK EDITIONS

For Tressa

CONTENTS

IT'S ALL IN THE FAMILY

Life's Best Perfumes

We homemakers take for granted so many of the homely little perfumes of living. Yet the nose continually offers us small delights all day long.

There are, of course, the usual pleasant aromas of baking. Meats roasting. Cakes and pies and gingerbread in the oven. The heady richness of anything made with chocolate. Fresh bread cooling. But here are some more that give me a tingle:

The tang of orange or lemon or grapefruit rinds being ground in a disposer in the sink...

The fragrant froth of liquid dishwashing soaps as you soak a pan of silver, or suds out a pair of hose...

The pungent stab of ammonia added to cleaning water...

The sour bite of vinegar being poured on a salad...

Today's laundry smells are nice smells too. (In contrast to the heavy gray odor of clothes being steamed in a boiler in the good old days—my nomination for one of the most dismal smells in the world.) So few of us dry clothes outdoors any more that we miss the smell of sun-sweet linens being taken down from the line; sheets especially. But today's detergents do their best to compensate.

There is a certain sweetness to clothes being

lifted from machine to dryer. Warm to your touch, and wrung damp but not dripping, they have a living quality about them, the scent of life. And later, when you take them hot and fluffy from the dryer, the clean sweetness still clings.

Ironing smells are nice smells too. Toasty, somehow. And most of the spray starches are delicately scented.

And what can equal the wonderful smell of children? . . . A baby after its bath . . . A little girl just shampooed . . . Small boys in from play, with the scent of all outdoors on their skin, along with the grubbiness . . . Even the musky odor of sweat shirts and tennis shoes when they get older . . . And oh, the heady loveliness of a daughter dressing for a date!

No, life's dearest perfumes aren't kept in expensive bottles on a dressing table.

A Fledgling Florence Nightingale

I think a bit of a nurse lurks in every woman.

The instinct to tend, to medicate and mother manifests itself even when we are small. A nursing kit is a must for every little girl. Just as doctor sets go automatically to little boys. But boys are generally less persistent in their desire to attend the ill. They graduate quickly into games more strenuous than poking a playmate to see where he hurts and feeding him candy pills. And not many small boys aspire to be doctors; they want to be firemen when they grow up, or policemen or astronauts.

But rare is the daughter who doesn't dream at some time of becoming a nurse. This honorable profession leads every what-do-you-want-to-be? poll. A girl loves the costume—apron and perky cap, the vision of taking temperatures, the authority and the cheery sweetness: "How are you feeling today? Let me rub your back." Until this vision is crowded out by others (or she faces the realities of training) almost every true female fancies herself a fledgling Florence Nightingale.

And she never quite outgrows it. From nursing sick dolls and pets she eventually graduates to nursing people, whether she works in hospital or home. Certainly mothers must be ready to be nurses at any hour. . . .

Women learn the mysterious methods of nursing in many ways. Through trial and error and advice from friends and reading books. But I think that fundamentally nature equips us with an instinctive wisdom, along with that vital necessity, tenderness. The deep concern instilled by nature keys us into action, sharpens our wits. Nature somehow tells us what to do. What's more, nature makes us want to do it.

When one of our family is hurt or ill, however inconvenient it may be, however weary we are, something swells up in us that is almost akin to joy. We are little girls again, fixing trays, cutting flowers, fluffing up pillows, reading to the patient, adjusting the blinds so that he or she can sleep. But no longer are we playing nurse in a pretty apron with a cute little cap to wear. This is for real. And the sense of secret drama is linked to a subtle sense of achievement: We've become what we always said we'd be some day—a nurse!

Preview of American Womanhood

Don't tell me most girls today are selfish young sophisticates who'll make poor wives and mothers. To the contrary, those we know are demonstrating some of the qualities of American womanhood right now—particularly in their gracious way with little girls.

The older daughter of some friends comes to visit, and you have her room ready. But seeing the shy, starry-eyed look of your little girl, the guest invites, "Oh, can't Melanie sleep with me? I'd just love to have her." And you hear them chatting and giggling in the night like contemporaries.

"She promised to write to me," your child announces, haunting the mailbox after she leaves. And you warn, "Oh, but she's awfully busy getting ready for her wedding. Don't count on it."

Then, as much to your delight as hers, the letter comes. And the little package, containing a doll dress fashioned out of the same material as that of the bridesmaids, and a sample of the wedding dress and veil! . . .

Another girl on a neighboring farm has been teaching our daughter to ride. "And let her come over any time she wants to give the horses a workout," she generously invites. And when the eager child appears, the busy teenager will leave off studying or preparations for a party to round up the favorite mare, help with the bridle and saddling. . . .

A college girl who's studying to be a vet pops in to check on the family pets—and her small admirer. "Come on home with Mom and me for dinner and the movies," she frequently includes her. And now that this young lady is being married too, she says, "I've just got to figure out a way for her to be in the wedding. She's too young to be a bridesmaid, too old for a flower girl—maybe we can invent a role for a middle-sized girl.". . .

Last year two Cherry Blossom Princesses not only gave her their autographs, but both of them wrote and sent their pictures, in answer to her letter. And their notes were kind and gay and charming, duplicating the X's for kisses she had sent.

Surely this is a mark not only of their maturity, but of some innate graciousness that will make them charming and gentle women.

A Family Test

The true test of a family is trouble. Will it be shattered by this grave blow, or will it survive to become even stronger than before?

Under the first impact it may stagger and falter,

and for a brief appalling moment feel its own structure slipping, its very fate in doubt.

But quickly then the good family recovers, unites, feels itself somehow stronger than before. Qualities unsuspected in its own members come rushing to the fore: the ability to understand, to weigh and analyze a problem and advise, the willingness to share, the capacity for sacrifice.

Members formerly at odds may be drawn together in the common bond of helping to save and solve this thing which threatens the precious whole. Goodness and kindness cement the cracks, tighten the slipping bonds.

If a family can meet trouble together and overcome it, then nothing can overcome that family. And each of its members will be able to cope with his own life a little better than before.

An Emergency Demands a Man

My favorite neighbor says: "Have you ever noticed how heroic husbands are in a crisis? Men seem just made for emergencies.

"They know what to do and they don't waste time doing it.

"They haven't a qualm about calling an ambulance, a fire engine, or even the police.

"Maybe they actually like these big dramatic strokes that a woman backs off from. Anyway, let a child get hurt, most dads are a tower of strength.

"Or let one's child get in a jam, or even serious trouble—it's usually dad who rushes to the rescue, not only with money but moral support. So many times when a woman would scold, or cry, or just fold up.

"But have you also noticed how a woman handles a hundred little crises day in and day out? How she can be patient and wise and equal to a whole parade of trials a man just couldn't stand?

"Maybe that explains it. Men rise to the big occasion because by then a woman's all used up!"

'I'll Never Love Anyone but You'

Dialogue with a son:

"Hey, don't touch the dial! I want to be sure and listen to that radio station all evening."

"How come?"

"Well, I called in and asked them to dedicate a song from me to Ann. She always listens while she's doing the dishes, and boy will she be thrilled!"

"How about Betsy? I thought you were taking her to the movies Saturday. Doesn't she listen to that station too?"

"Oh, my gosh, that's right," he gasps. Then, "I know what—I'll call the station right now and have the announcer dedicate the song to both of them!"

"By the way, what song is it?"

"I'll Never Love Anyone But You."

A Woman and Her Floor

Floors are the platforms of life. The foundations. What a wonderful thing is a floor!

"How many floors?" we ask of any new building. And count them—those shelves that often climb like a child's blocks until it seems they must topple. But no, they are secured, and what was empty space becomes a soaring city where people love, laugh, live, are born or snatched from death in operations. All because of floors.

And our houses—our upstairs, our downstairs, our floors. Daily we sweep them, scrub or wax them. And across them our children run as we cry, "Don't track my floor!" Or, "Stop cluttering up my floor."

My floor! Firm beneath your feet as you traverse your female kingdom. A care, but such a comfort. And sometimes as you cross it, vacuuming, straightening—memories go marching through doorways into the house of your childhood. You see your mother on these selfsame daily journeys, sweeping, dusting, picking up.

And you remember the hot nights of summer when people used to get up and sleep on the floor. It was cooler there; if any breeze stirred it would find you.

It was fun, anyway, to sleep on the floor. It was the most exciting part of having company. The company got the beds, and the children could scramble into these gay nests that your mother made up for you on the floor.

"Now all of you be quiet. Go to sleep," adults would order. But how could you? For it was like camping, hard as the ground. You giggled and squirmed and whispered. You could feel the rug prickling when you flung out a hand, and smell its dusty tang. The legs of the furniture reared up like strange beasts, ominous and thrilling. . . . Even today, in air conditioned houses with plenty

of beds for everybody, youngsters often tease, "Oh, please let us sleep on the floor!"

Maybe because a child, being small, feels close to the floor. The floor is the child's world. He plays there, sits there to watch television, to cut, color, work puzzles. He feels secure there; he can't fall off, and he can spread out—his possessions, or himself.

Some of us never outgrow this. We still like to sit on the floor. And a floor is a grand place to rest. A bed is sometimes simply too full of life—we spend so many hours in bed, awake, asleep or dreaming.

But a floor is impersonal, soothing as a country plain. You can stretch to your outer limits on the floor. You can exercise or just lie there letting tensions flow out across its bland plateau.

And floors are so convenient. I like to pile things on the floor; to have a stack of books or a basket of sewing on the floor beside a chair. Or to sort papers on a floor's generous expanse.

Desks are often like subway trains, books and papers crowding and spilling all over each other. But ah, the lovely aisles of space those books and papers can enjoy when you spread them out and really see them, on the floor.

I love a floor's silence, and its small, half-human creaks.

Curiously, a floor is both impersonal—and yet richly human. Every floor we walk upon becomes for a little while an exciting stage upon which we act out the drama of our lives . . . I love a floor!

The Cleaning Spree

There is something about weathering the emotional storms of a family that inspires many a woman to go on a cleaning spree.

It is as if, during all the winds of chaos and conflict, the house itself has taken a battering. Or perhaps, in the bright sweet after-calm, we see it with new awareness—and are touched by its own mute confusions; its problems that too had been mounting daily and patiently. The cluttered cupboards. The pantry, the closets that have gradually gotten into such disarray.

"You poor things," you think. "You too need me!"

Energies you had thought used up in the emotional arena, now spring to the forefront physically. Relieved of other problems, situations that had seemed critical resolved (this child or that bailed out of trouble, this financial complexity disentangled, this dire misunderstanding over), what relief, what sudden joy!

You can lick this landscape of simpler things with one hand tied. It is yours to rearrange, refurbish, rebuild.

Out with all those useless items that have been cluttering up the place so long. A new courage assails you—get rid of things, throw the burdensome away. And a wonderful lightness follows, a sense of bright release. Because these acts and decisions are not life-compelling; they involve only objects. And the sense of achievement is immediate and concrete.

You see its evidence before you—the glasses neatly shining on their shelves, the closets tidy, the dark accusing corners now cleanly sweet. Compared to coping with people, how remarkably easy to deal with a mere house!

Mothers of Daughters

What do women do without daughters?

I mean what do they do for raincoats and scarves and belts and eyelash curlers? . . .

Gather with almost any covey of women and you can generally spot the mothers of daughters, teen-age and beyond. They are usually the ones in the most make-up and wearing the youngest, gayest clothes.

Compliment someone on that attractive leather jumper or her green eyeshadow and she's likely to explain, "It's Toni's," or "Ginny left it when she went away to school," or "Jane wanted me to try it."

The mother of daughters has two motives: one,

she feels economically obliged to wear the cast-offs. That perfectly good lingerie that needs a strap; those hose whose runners won't show under boots. Those boots that the child has outgrown (vitamins give them big feet). Or merely that party dress her daughter's already worn twice and doesn't dare be seen in again!

Two, is the daughter's coaching. "Hold in your stomach. Let me do something about your hair." "I'll show you how to put on false eyelashes." At a recent wedding I was amused to notice that virtually all the mothers of older girls were wearing eyeliner. Whereas, few of the young new mothers were. Either they were too busy to bother or simply not inspired.

We knew a mousy little woman who didn't be-

gin to blossom until her daughter went away to college. The transformation was miraculous.

She inherited all those clothes, and had to reduce to fit them.

And she got to experimenting with all that half-used makeup. The results were so striking she got herself a wig.

In less than a year she was so changed her own husband sometimes wondered if he'd come to the wrong house.

Not always, of course, but sometimes the mothers of mere males get thick and masculine themselves. "With nothing but men to look at it's easy to go into a slump," one of them told me. "It helps to have a model around."

On the other hand, my sister Gwen, who never had anything but sons, is extra-conscious of glamor. "They think of me as their girl. And I want to keep them interested."

She, like a lot of women—career women, or wealthy women—just goes out and buys what she wants. Such women also go to hairdressers and salons and fashion shows to keep up. But all this takes money.

Mothers of daughters don't always have the money, but they have something even better—the models! Plus a dependable source of supply—the castoffs.

A Psychological Lift

What did women do before beauty parlors? I don't mean merely about their hair (they rolled it up on kid curlers or crimped it with an iron heated over a kerosene lamp). Or their nails (they filed and buffed them and kept them clean). Or their faces (which they creamed by night, washed by day, and patted delicately with rice powder).

No, I mean something more: the psychological lift a woman gets from simply walking into a familiar place and, in more ways than one, taking down her hair.

What did they do without an Edna to talk to (or a Jackie, or a Pearl, a Pat or a Louise?) Who filled that peculiarly feminine function of attending to their tresses to the tune of sheer woman-talk?

"How are the children?" you ask of Edna, and she asks, in turn, of yours. And the mutual woes and wonders of family cares are exchanged. "Have you heard about the Joneses? They're moving back," she informs you, wielding a vigorous brush before dunking you in the suds. (And believe it or not, the news that one hears at one's neighborhood hairdresser's is usually good news.)

"Why, that's wonderful," you say, both of the Joneses and the luxuriant ministrations to your scalp.

How many hours have you spent in such discussions over the years you've been coming to her or the other girls in this shop that is like an adjunct of home? And no matter how often the prodigal patron goes wandering, the light is always burning in the window for your return.

After those economical streaks when you decide it's nonsense to spend all that money, and if you'll just wear it simple you can shampoo it yourself and set it at night. The times when, recklessly, you've even whacked it off (for what woman can resist the sheer daring of trying to cut her own hair now and then?), and come limping back begging, "do something, anything to make me look civilized again!"

Or the times when, contrarily, you've heard of this shockingly expensive but très chic little man who's supposed to make you look so glamorous your own family won't know you. (Only that's the trouble, they don't! In fact, they scream.)

Or the times when you trail in hopelessly bleached and baked and parched after a summer at the shore.

Some women prefer male hairdressers, true. If a man's really good, he's terrific. And there is something flattering about turning yourself over to masculine magic. As if he must have some secret unknown to mere females. As if perhaps like the fairy prince his very touch must make you beautiful.

But the relation between women and women is an instinctive and timeless thing. And I have sometimes wondered what there is about this act performed by one woman for another that makes them feel so close?

Is it perhaps some lost luxuriant echo of an era and a way of life when many women had personal maids? Or does it go back to the days when you were a little girl with your head on your mother's knee, knowing the unutterable drowsy comfort of having her brush your hair until it shone? Of the security and tenderness you felt as her strong fingers rolled it up in rags for curls, or expertly braided your pigtails and topped it off with a bow?

Whatever it is, it's become as permanent as, well—a permanent—on the American scene.

NATURE'S GLORIES

Morning Birds

How impudent are morning birds! How annoy-ingly gay. Tired, needing sleep, you hear them starting up sometimes outside your window, like insistent little alarm clocks that you can't shut off or hurl away. Trilling and cheeping and shrill-ing their glad little cries. Running scales. Ringing bells of brightness. Chiming.

How they carry on, unaware of the head that plunges into the pillow. Or the being who rises, stalks to the window, prepared to shoo or shout "Oh, go away!"

Only you cannot. No, you cannot. For the day itself is too giddily joyful too. Fresh, untasted. New and sparkling. The sky a cool pink-tinged blue.

The trees are all atwinkle in the coming sun. Their branches dip slightly under the fragile singers. Leaves tremble as, with a spurt of wings, a glimmer of color, an oriole or a cardinal soars away.

By contrast—how silently. How effortless the lift of wings. How totally unresistant. Their mo-tion is like the spontaneous spill of music from their throats. Birds are so relaxed. They sound and seem so free, so happy, because they don't fight their surroundings. They simply flow into them.

And now you think: How peaceful are morning birds. How restful.

For their joy is contagious. You feel it beginning to dance and sparkle within you as your own resistance gives way. You want to laugh. You want to join their bright chorus and go singing into the new day.

Oh, but you're not a bird, remember? The day will be complex. Filled with phone calls, duties, problems, jobs that nobody, man, or bird, could effortlessly fly through. But maybe the birds have been little emissaries to prepare you. "Sing if you can" they may have been saying. "But when you can't, remember our silence too."

Mother Nature's Green

Green is a stubborn color. It clings to the landscape, no matter what the season.

Even in early December, when most of the trees are stripped, their silver-gray branches and trunks are still adorned with frail little errant vines of triumphant green.

The pines are furred in their vivid green needles. The willows wear a fluff of delicate yellow-green fronds, like lingering ghosts of spring.

The lake at our summer cabin reflects, in its

olive-drab waters, the leaning shadows of the trees in a dusky muted green.

The sky, however, wears a face of changing colors. Especially of an evening after a mild day. Clouds ranging from solid shining white to the purple of plums are piled castle-high as you drive through the countryside.

Between them the burning apple of the sun sinks swiftly, leaving its ruddy stain. While behind them fanlike rays shine upward, as if pointing to a heavenly kingdom, or splay downward like spokes of a golden wheel.

By six o'clock the dark clouds have taken possession, though here and there a timid star parts the curtains to peer through.

The sky keeps rearranging itself all evening.

We take our coffee down on the dock after supper, and sit beside the water, rimmed round by the wooded hills, watching the sky shuffling its light clouds and its dark ones in a game of starry hide and seek, with glimpses now and then of a tiny nail-new moon.

And gradually all the dark clouds give way before the light ones. The horizon, the whole sky glows with a pearly gray light that is more like the light of daybreak.

And though the air is cold, shafts of warmth float over us and down, as if a last gift from the sun's remembered wheel.

And it is mysterious and strange—evening yet morning, chill yet warm, winter yet spring, the bald bare time, yet the time of the persistent green.

The Wet and Wonderful Fair

All week you've been telling the family, "Wait, we can go to the fair tomorrow," for every day there's been company—or rain. Then it is the last day, last night, and still raining, and mass gloom prevails.

"But we always go to the fair," the children wail.

"That's right; surely we can miss this one."

At this heresy even your husband is shocked. "Can't we go at least for supper? It might be even more fun in the rain."

So boots are found, such sketchy rain gear as you keep at the cabin, one lone umbrella, and off you go, expecting to be the only idiots abroad. "Surely you don't charge admission the last night in the rain?" your husband kids the boy at the gate.

"For rain we charge extra," he laughs.

And perhaps they should. For the colored lights are wheels and banners of misted loveliness as you slog across the wet grass; their rainbows are mirrored in the puddles. Streams pour from the canvas stands like silver fringe.

The rain makes orchestration for the brave and merry tinkling of the merry-go-round, one of the few rides in motion. The children have their pick of the wealth of horses that seem to leap and glide with an added shining splendor, up and down, up and down.

The midway is neither crowded nor deserted. Those who trudge its muddy passage beam upon each other in a spirit of holiday and folly. There is something patiently bemused about even the pitchmen waving their gaudy enticements. The freaks huddling under a dripping awning—the fat lady, the tattooed man—smile down as if sharing some merry secret. The torch of the flame thrower casts a coppery reflection and sizzles and sputters in the wetness.

It is cozy in the great livestock sheds. The huge pink hogs are sleeping like babies in their pens while overhead the rain drums down. The children try to bury their hands in the wool of a sheep. "You couldn't spank a lamb, he wouldn't feel it!" In the poultry barn roosters crow, hens cluck. Baby ducks are trying to catch a trickle of water with open bills. The good tangy farmyard smell is heightened by the rain.

And so is the fragrance of frying onions. You line up at a counter and order hamburgers, great sizzling platters of chicken. The orangeade, sweating with cold, tastes like this nowhere else.

At last, warmed and full, with your hands filled with trinkets, you head for the car, pausing as always for popcorn, taffy apples, cotton candy.

"Wait, I'll put a raincoat on it," says the fat little cotton candy man, wrapping the rosy puff in cellophane.

Shielding this plunder as best you can, you scurry on through a new downpour. The lights behind you shine merrily on. You can still hear the brave bright tinkle of the merry-go-round.

Spring Picnics

The trees are tentative and hesitant with their leaves, holding them back like something precious that we don't quite deserve and will take for granted all too soon. Though some are already exhibiting their tender little green umbrellas.

The willows beside the water are a delicate froth of green. The maples are pink. The pines have a strong dark feathering. The redbuds bloom.

You fill the boat with children one day and travel far up the lake, flanked on all sides by the trees. Their trunks rise like pencil strokes toward the pinkish sparkling of the leaves. The light of a pale sun weaves through them, pure and shining. Rocks explode, gray-green, covered with a silvery lichen. They too catch the silvery pinkish light of spring. And over all hangs the fragile canopy of the almost-ready leaves...

Birds dart into the secret crevasses of the greater rocks along the shore. Turtles are stacked like saucers on a log. A child cries "Look—look at the flowers!" Clumps of bluebells—the farther you go the more you are aware of them—blooming in modest yet glorious abundance in neglected expanses of muddy banks and little paths and seldom-traveled roads. "Let's stop and pick some."

"Wait till after the picnic. They'd only wilt."

You tie up at a favorite spot beneath some pines and spread your blankets. You are sheltered by a vast singing cathedral, slippery floored, smelling of incense. Its spires catch the clouds. The lake reflects its grandeur—and its cows, grazing on a near bank.

You eat slightly cold hot dogs from your basket

and drink slightly warm cokes. The children toss the scraps to the fish, but the dog dives in after them. In and out of the water she plunges, then swims, intrigued, toward the gloomily watching cows.

"Come back, come back!" everybody shouts. "Mr. Keyes won't let us picnic here if you chase his cows."

She hesitates, in a torment of temptation, then stands quivering on the float, challenging them with every inch of body, tail, ears and bark.

"Cows look so sad," someone remarks. "Do you suppose they'd be happy if we took them a hot dog?"

At length you shove off and return, pausing to pull up for a branch of redbuds—scarcely worth the effort for the tiny red beads begin shedding, especially when clambered over by a dripping dog. But ah, the bluebells! Worth the climb over slippery rocks and tangled roots. In the stilly pinkness of the low flat woods they stand, tall yet faintly drooping, like shy girls attired for the party yet afraid to dance.

Their stalks are pliant, their leaves limp green velvet, their flowers tiny bells of mingled blue and pink. Hosts of them longing to be found.

You gather armloads of these lovelies and bring them home and put them in pots and pitchers.

They stand with bowed heads, beautiful, clusters of lavender ladies in chiffon.

The Wild and Lovely Light

Some days seem especially dedicated to light. You awake in the morning to feel this gay exuberance —the way you feel the presence of a vivid and enticing personality.

It is not heat. Nor exactly the sun itself. No, no, it is something more, an essence, an unexpected gift, a benediction. It is simply—light.

It pours through the windows urging, "Look, come look!" It rains in golden shafts through the mysterious green banks of the trees. Usually dark, shrouded in a secret society of shadows, they are ripped wide by the laughing light, denuded in brilliance, exposed. All their leaves twinkle and flirt, their twigs cavort, silver-fingered. Their high green sky-brushing heads are hatted in proud golden plumes.

The light is a prancing presence, a live thing full of its own shimmering joy and artistry.

It races ahead on the gravel road, transforming its sand to a treasury of dusty silver-gold. It blazes on the window-glass of houses and windshields, and the steel bodies of cars. It flings itself headlong on water—pool, stream, lake or sea. There it goes wild, flashing and flaunting and flinging itself about in a bacchanalian ecstasy. While in the center, the sun lies blandly captured, rocking and tilting this way and that, like some unconcerned god or vast burning flower.

The Angel Bird

Each year the herons come—stately steel-blue beings who nest in the rushes across from the cabin, and stalk the fishes on slender legs. They fly with their long necks arched inward, emitting their curious cry, "Frahnk, frahnk!"

There is always mystery and excitement about any large bird. These almost people-sized creatures who can lift themselves so magically and soar off into the sky. As if they could carry you with them if you made your longing clear and they so willed.

Then there are the bitterns, a chunkier smaller species, the brown of the weeds. But loveliest of all the herons is the white one which descends once a season, like a visiting celebrity, and usually alone.

"Mommy, guess what? An angel flew by my window this morning!" a child exclaims. And so it seems. For there is something unearthly about that white span of wings against the vivid blue sky. Something that speaks of purity, joy and peace, coasting down.

How placidly it perches upon the piece of driftwood it has chosen; the silver of the sun-bleached wood, the snowy body, a statue reflected on the water. How patiently it stands in the shallows, or walks the sands with slow elegant grace. It is oblivious to our admiring gaze. Yet sometimes the children are convinced it dips its wings to us, going by. And sometimes it cuts so close to the cabin you could reach out and touch it, so it seems.

You know better. It would be like trying to touch an angel. It would be like holding in your hands for one brief, enthralling instant the bright bird of happiness. It would be too much.

But whenever anyone announces its arrival, or calls out, "The white heron's still here," it is like a good omen. You feel that for a small and lovely while you have a heavenly guardian.

Snow Picture

Beauty in your own backyard. . . .

A cardinal spurts like a streak of blood above a world banked bright with snow. A usually saucy bluejay cowers beneath a bush that is bowed with the weight of its furry wrap. . . .

Icicles, like enormous shining lances, hang from the eaves. . . .

Grudgingly the children concede defeat before the voice on the radio. "School will be open—." Bundled and booted, they trudge off, with backward glances at the sleds upended against the garage. . . .

Doing the breakfast dishes, you look out to see your neighbor, a young rector, hauling his little girl about. Spying you and your own littlest at the window, they both look up and wave. . . .

He wears an overcoat and a collegiate looking porkpie hat. His white teeth flash; his black vest and white strip of collar are vivid in the glittering light. His cherry-cheeked child wears a tasseled cap. . . .

Your own excited offspring is stuffed into her red snowsuit and bonnet and little red mittens. Your husband, home for the day, gets into his wraps and galoshes and carries her outside. She too is enthroned on a sled, and the two men, laughing, pull the two solemn fat red babies about. . . .

Yours tumbles off and stands crying, dusted with snow like a doughnut. Her father brushes her off and the minister lifts her onto the other sled beside her friend. Grinning and panting a little he goes tramping off to the rectory so that his wife can admire them from her window.

Your husband takes up his snow shovel, and its bright music rings on the cold tingling air as he scoops the walk. Feeling you can do no less, you don boots and scarf and jacket and attack the drifted porch with a lop-sided golden stub of a broom.

Waters Are Like People

Waters are like people. They have different qualities.

The ocean has a different character than a tranquil lake or a rollicking mountain stream. It is powerful, majestic, and often ominous. It roars of its power, ceaseless, eternal, heavy with ships and sails and secrets, dark with mystery. Its very feel and taste inspire your respect. It is strong with salt, and often cold; it bites and slogs you and has a tingling sting.

Mountain streams often have this same vigorous

39

quality. A tangible strength, bracing and tonicky. They boil and bounce noisily along, foaming over rocks, pitching down a precipice, confident of their own importance as they rush to join forces with river or sea.

Then there are lazy, gentle little country creeks. They laugh and murmur and caress your wading feet. They are in no hurry—lovely, indolent things. Butterflies hover above them, cows drowse in their muddy shallows, minnows dart, frogs croak, gnats and little birds sing.

There are differences between lakes, as well. The Iowa lake on which I was raised is big and noisy and seldom still. Storm Lake, the Indians christened its windy waters. It bashes and smashes and carries on so I think it must fancy itself first cousin to the sea. . . . Though on a still night it can be regally placid, paved with a blazing silver path that leads straight to the moon. . . . Its embrace is sometimes harsh, sometimes soft as velvet. It is a lake of many moods.

The Virginia lake on which we have our summer cabin is called Lake Jackson, near Manassas. It is man-made, formed by damming up two streams, Broad Run and Cedar Run.

It is more like a wide but beautiful river, meandering some ten miles through wooded hills and meadows. It has no illusions about itself; the roughest it ever gets is when a breeze ruffles its silver feathers, or a speedboat cuts an impressive swath. It is like a gracious woman, modestly aware of her charms: the fish, the friendly people, the graceful weekend ballet of water skiers.

Its waters are infinitely soft. Silken soft. We wash our hair in them. And to plunge into them, whatever the weather, is to know a gentle melting, a liquid caress, soothing as sleep.

Granddaddy Long Legs

A granddaddy longlegs appears as you sit on a sunny dock fishing one day, an eye on the water, the other on the Sunday paper.

Silent and weightless, he emerges at the edge of the paper and clings there, an arched and tentative creature that you could abandon with the flick of a finger, or destroy with a step. Yet how delicate and fine a fellow he is, with his many marvelous legs and his tentacles that reach out all aquiver and his eyes that seem to regard you, friendly and wary. As if awaiting your verdict, and knowing already that you wouldn't have the heart to harm so charming a visitor.

Reassured, his invisible feet begin to stroke the paper, as if feeling its smooth texture. Then he makes his graceful way across it, his body the exact gray color of the newsprint. He is like his own airy headline, his own fine moving story. And as you watch him in idle fascination, he halts and suddenly stands on his head!

You laugh in disbelief. "Look, come look," you long to summon people, to witness his dear, foolish behavior. For he is like a small boy who must have an audience. He not only perches there impressively upon his head a few seconds, he turns a somersault! Then rights himself and repeats the whole performance.

Again you long to call out to others, but there's nobody about—and besides you fear lest his temperament be as fine as his threadlike feelers and he will scurry away. You can only sit, lone witness to his art.

In a minute he proceeds across the paper, pausing at this story or that, as if to scan them, nod gravely, wag a finger or his head. Finally he reaches the paper's edge and balances there swinging to and fro like an acrobat whose act is concluded and now performs some final flourishes before dropping from the net.

He vanishes under the dock. You see him no more. But every time you think of him you feel a laugh welling up inside, you almost want to applaud.

The Bonfire

Beauty in your own backyard. . . .

In the lavender twilight your husband is raking the leaves. They flow after the rake's arched tines in a tumbling tide of silvery bronze.

The lights of neighboring houses come on and touch them with an added dimension of living light. They are dry yet silken, rustling like an old-fashioned lady's petticoats, shining, shining, as the fork reaches out for them and draws them insistently toward the country roadside hollow to be burned.

The smoke breathes upward in soft, lazy puffs. But as the fresh offering is added and stirred, it leaps in bright spurtings of orange flame. He is silhouetted there beside it, barely discernible, like a dark spirit conjured up by its heat. He stands bending and stirring and stroking, before these tents of flame.

Their pointed tops reach skyward. Sharp fingers stretch out from the tents, flinging sparks, or trying greedily to catch them. The sparks make a bright swirling glitter against the lilac dusk. And the leaves fly and twist upward too, as if to reclaim the space from which they came. They circle bird-like above the fire, before falling to their fate.

Children come rushing up, begging to help. They dance madly around the fire, poking it with sticks. "A torch, a torch!" one cries, lifting a burning brand and prancing about with it, implike.

"Come on, now, stop playing and help," their father orders, surrendering a rake. The fire clucks and chatters and roars in a merry rejoicing as it gobbles the fresh offering of leaves.

A small new circlet of moon smiles down. It lies a little to the west, leaning on its back, like a child itself, kept in a thin little golden crib, wanting to join the fun.

Mornings Are Special

My mother always loved the morning.

I know a lot of people do. But with her morning was special. I can't say that she never woke up cross or troubled, I'm sure she often did. But what I remember most are those mornings when she was so full of hope and joy and enthusiasm, bubbling with bright plans for the day.

"Get up," she would call from the foot of the stairs. "Oh, do get up now, come on—it's such a beautiful day!"

And as we burrowed deeper, she would launch into a veritable paean of description: "The sun is shining so brightly and the birds are singing. Just listen to them, I can hear a mockingbird. And there's a nest of orioles in the lilac bushes, there goes one now!"

She would then produce more practical reasons: "I'm going to bake and clean and that garden needs weeding, so come on, you can help, I need you. But really it's so lovely out it'll be a pleasure, a person can accomplish so much on a beautiful day!"

By noon her enthusiasm had begun to wane, by midafternoon her hopes and energies were definitely dragging. No doubt her offspring's failing to share her zest to get up and enjoy the world (and its jobs) had a lot to do with this. But she was definitely what would today be labeled "A Morning Person."

And so am I. Morning is so new, unshabby and unsoiled. Morning is like a brand-new garment fresh out of the box. You want to try it on. To wear it! No matter what its color—sunny or gray —garbed in morning nothing seems impossible. By afternoon you're used to it, the day seems adequate, it covers you, but is no longer exciting.

By evening you're tired; the day's score is being tallied up, and sometimes you're not sure it was worth it. What did you accomplish? Nothing. Or seldom as much as you intended to. Sometimes you shrink back in dismay from the errors you have made, the miseries endured. (How could morning have so betrayed you—morning with its promise!)

Or if the promises have been fulfilled—your achievements please you, there has been excitement, unexpected pleasure—then, yes, evening can be lovely, looking back on it. But it's over when you go to bed. There's no calling back the day—the bad of it to be somehow changed, or the good of it either.

For morning people it is only in the morning that life is so entirely yours, unused, unspoiled, filled with the thrilling mystery of what lies ahead; and yet that is, right now, this moment, so beautiful, so intensely satisfying.

For me heaven will be like that. And when a voice calls, "Get up now, come on, it's morning!" I won't mind a bit.

How to Meet Defeat

There are four ways to meet defeat:

You can despair, go into a spasm of protesting grief.

You can leave the scene, do something you enjoy in an attempt to forget and compensate.

You can stay where you are, but attack a different project.

Or you can return to the original battleground and fight harder.

The first course, if prolonged, is dangerous. It only makes defeat seem worse, and defeats you further by leaving you limp and weak. I think a little bit of this is necessary, however. A flood of anger, or of tears, gets rid of emotion that maybe needs releasing.

What next? Preferably back to work. If not on the original undertaking, then another. Flying off on a shopping spree, a trip, or to meet a friend may sometimes be wonderful therapy and give you perspective, but escape, however welcome, only postpones the hour of reckoning.

The best course of all, I think, is a bit of all four: Cry a little, pray a little, play a little. Have lunch with someone you enjoy.

Then back to the battleground, riding the self-same horse that threw you. Maybe he's in a tamer mood; or maybe you've gained in skill and strength. If not, put him firmly away and lock the stable door—at least for now.

The timing may not be right just now (or ever). In any case, don't waste precious energy grieving. There are plenty of other horses in the pasture. Pick one out and lasso it. The only way to really overcome defeat is to do the original better, or put something else worth doing in its place.

To Cherish

Surely one of the loveliest words in the marriage ceremony is "cherish." We don't hear it very often after that. People use it far less frequently than "love." And we don't even think much about it. For "cherish" is a shy kind of word, gentle and inconspicuous, not subject to discussion or magazine articles and songs.

Yet nothing is more vital to human happiness than—to be cherished. It means: "To hold dear. To treat with tenderness and affection; hence to nurture with care." How commonplace, and yet at the same time how exquisite.

You are foolish. You can't balance your checkbook, you overcharge things, you tell corny jokes, you sometimes yell. . . . And yet the family forgives you, laughs at you, makes allowances for you. Impossible though you are, you are dear to them. Cherished. . . .

You have to make a trip. There are countless complicated arrangements to be made. Who'll take care of the house? Who'll transport people various directions? . . . Don't worry; family, even friends, rise to help. For some odd reason they want this to be easy for you, and pleasant. You are cherished. . . .

You get the flu. But you can't get the flu, not

with everything else! But you are put sternly to bed. You hear them managing without you. Tiptoeing in now and then to bring you a pill, or orange juice, or just check on how you are. Soothing, "Now get to sleep and forget everything." And drifting off, the sweet awareness comes over you: "This is what it's all about, really—to be cherished."

There's nothing romantic about it. Nothing passionate, or dramatic, nothing intellectual or adventurous, or a lot of things women sometimes long for. But how peaceful, how wonderful, how —important. To be cared about, looked after, held dear. To be nurtured, to be cherished.

It's Important to Be Nice

There's an old saying: "It's nice to be important, but it's more important to be nice."

But just what is a nice person? . . . Not "nice" in the properly dressed up for Sunday School sense, or too nicey-nice to participate in the vigorous business of life—but nice as a human being. Nice to be with. Nice "to come home to" as the song goes. Nice to know.

First, the nice person is usually pleasant. He isn't always crying the blues, about himself or the

world. His ailments are generally his private property.

And the nice person is kind. A nice guy will give you a boost instead of a knock. And he's nice not only to your face, but behind your back. To be truly nice is thorough, it goes deep.

That's why the nice person can be trusted. You know he'd never betray you, sell you short, use you to reach his own ends.

And he's somebody you can count on. He'll not make promises he doesn't intend to keep. If he says "I'll do it," you know he means it. And if he fails, there'll be a darn good reason. Which troubles him sometimes more than it does you.

But he has the happy capacity of being helpful on the spot. Thinking of ways to give you a lift to church, to the supermarket, or toward your private star. He'll make phone calls, write letters, on your behalf. He'll give you tips and leads and ideas. And the best part of all this is he doesn't keep score. He doesn't expect to be repaid.

He's nice because he wants to be!

The nice guys are not necessarily the most successful. They lack the fierce ambition and ruthlessness that it sometimes takes to get ahead. But they are rich in friends, rich in inner satisfaction. For they enjoy that loveliest of all rewards, the sheer pleasure that comes with doing something decent, kind, generous, considerate. . . .

And when nice people do get to the top they have an added dimension that adds to their lustre and their lasting qualities. For people who are fundamentally nice are secure, they have no need to be discourteous or forbidding. Thus it is true, that the most famous and successful are generally the nicest to deal with.

But whatever one's status, how good when people can say of us: "Now, there's a very nice person," or, "He's a darned nice guy!"

If Only

Two of life's futile words are "If only—"

"If only we'd bought that land when we could have gotten it so cheap we'd be wealthy now.". . . "If only we hadn't taken this trip the car accident wouldn't have happened.". . . If only you'd taken a different job, married a different person, gone to a different school—how much simpler, easier, more rewarding life would be. Or so it seems through the rosy glasses of hindsight.

And yet, how wrong. Because, just as nobody can predict what's around the bend of his choices —the opportunities, the mistakes—neither can he foresee what worse fate might have befallen had he chosen differently. As Emerson reminds us in his essay on Compensation, everything has its price, nothing in life comes free.

The person you pine "if only" you'd married, might have been appallingly wrong. The riches gained by the "if only" property could have brought their own unimagined penalty. One thing sure, you'll never know! And they strew one's present paths with jagged stones.

They block our forward progress, they need-lessly bruise our feet.

The best any of us can do is to act within the framework of what seems at the moment right and wise, and take the consequences. Good or bad, they can't be changed by a single "if only." And "if only" the truth could be revealed to us—we'd probably be infinitely thankful for exactly what we have now!

Those Who Do

There are two kinds of people in this world: those who do and those who don't.

Those who participate, and those who observe. Those to whom things happen—and those who make things happen.

If you're bored, lonely, frustrated, maybe it's just because you—don't. Stop just watching other people play the games—learn how, join in. No matter if you're clumsy and uncertain at first, everybody is. Practice, and you'll improve.

Get a job. Or if you can't find a job you like (or hate the one you have) start a business! Put those slumbering ideas to work. Have the courage to plunge in.

Take a course in something that interests you. Or teach one! Nearly everybody has something in his background that makes him an expert, or could with a bit of concentrated brushing up.

It may be as erudite as Mayan art, as homelike

as how to bake a better loaf of bread—there are people eager to share your knowhow, and as you teach, your own interest is whetted afresh, you too learn!

Join a club—or get one going. Try out for a play—or write one. If you can't stand your present surroundings, or are merely bored and indifferent to them—renovate, redecorate, or move.

But for goodness sake do something! The very difficulties you encounter will be of interest; even if you should fail you will be a richer person in the coin of life's experience. And all the lives you touch as you reach out will be the richer, livelier too because of your efforts.

Get out of the bleachers and onto the playing field. Stop being just a spectator, join the team—or start it, coach it.

Make something happen!

The Helping Hand

Deep in most people there is an honest need to see other people well and happy. I think this urge is one of our strongest instincts. To love, to care for, to pet, to help.

Observing the way little folks bang each other over the head and struggle selfishly for toys, we overlook the many instances when they rush to each other's aid. A toddler falls out of his wagon, and a sister not much bigger runs to his howling side. "That's all right, honey," she soothes, "I'll help you." And she struggles to pick him up and lug him to Mother for mending.

Or another small child will press upon you or his contemporaries a lollipop, a box of crayons, a flower. And you hear youngsters of all ages proffering sage advice—about the best way to pull a tooth, fasten a pair of skates, solve a homework problem. And as they grow older this urge to aid and counsel intensifies.

Let's not be too quick to chalk this up to another instinct, the desire to feel important. It is equally important to the human species to sense that however weak, confused or erring he may be, he still can smooth the way for someone else on this often bewildering and hurtful journey.

With some people this urge is so compelling it

becomes dedication. They choose professions in which they devote their lives to the cause. With others it becomes an avocation; they are volunteers, part-time. "Do gooders," they are disparagingly sometimes labeled; a term that is surely coined from the stings of conscience. For when we ourselves neglect so basic an instinct, we often uneasily strike out.

But for most busy, everyday people the desire to help manifests itself in common, garden-variety advice. When we discover a bonus, a short-cut, a cure, a source of hope for anything—from bargains to beauty, from aching joints to ailing ovens, from family peace to peace of mind—we cannot keep the good news to ourselves. We are absolutely impelled to speak out.

And when the object of our concern is reluctant or indifferent, we feel a sense of frustration. "Please, at least try it!" we plead.

This concern for each other is innate. Rooted in this universal knowledge that we are really all one family. And whenever we can add to another's comfort or diminish another's pain, we are fulfilling a God-given obligation—to contribute to the sum of human happiness.

Elements of Joy

What are the elements of joy?

Love. Laughter. And things that are agreeable to the senses. All five of them, sight, smell, touch, taste, sound. We might add too—something that stirs the intellect, the aesthetically satisfying.

Many moments of life are enhanced by some of these. And there are times when all come to us in a package. One shining fusion of the many aspects of delight. And how good to be aware of it.

This happened recently, breakfasting on the cabin porch. How peaceful and pleasant this is, it occurred to me. Here, right now, this minute are surely all the elements of enjoyment:

Something good to eat. (The tray with its egg, its orange juice, its crisp toast and good rich coffee.)

Something pleasant to smell. (That same steaming coffee. . . . The fragrance of wet grass in the morning sun.)

Something beautiful to see. (The spikes of purple swamp hyacinths rising from water beginning to sparkle. . . . The trees bending toward their own reflections.)

Something nice to hear. (Birds were twittering and caroling. . . . An ax rang in nearby woods.)

Something to cuddle, to touch. (The cat sprang

onto the balcony from its night's meandering, then into my lap. Its fur was warm and soft, its dry pink sandpaper nose pleasant against the wrist. Rumbling with content, it settled down.)

Laughter. Something satisfying to both the mind and the spirit. (The book beside me was that rare combination—artistically written and genuinely funny. Was it perhaps that lingering sense of amusement and general intelligent well-being that brought this awareness on?)

Love. The consciousness of love. (Husband. Friends. Children.)

So there it all was, in one shining combination. Soon, I knew, to vanish. Yet how precious then and there! Worthy of notice.

And really so available to most of us so often. Not just married people with families—everyone.

For love includes anyone very dear to us. And he or she doesn't have to be present or lived with.

In fact these moments of enjoyment come mostly in times of solitude. It's hard to hear the music, sniff the fragrance, taste the essence, surrounded by voices clamoring for attention. Or in normal everyday experience something is amiss. (The toast is burned. The radio is blaring. Instead of a placid lake we gaze upon a cluttered living room. The laughter may actually cause angry tears.)

Yet some elements of enjoyment pervade almost every hour, if we only notice them. And on those rare occasions when they combine, if we acknowledge them, salute them, give thanks.

Set in Walbaum, a light open typeface
designed by Justus Erich Walbaum (1768-1839),
a type founder at Goslar and at Weimar.
Printed on Hallmark Eggshell Book paper.
Designed by Bruce Baker.